LET'S LEARN
SPANISH

Written and edited by
Janet De Saulles and
Carol Watson
Illustrated by
Kim Woolley and
Shelagh McNicholas

COURAGE
B O O K S

An imprint of
Running Press
Philadelphia • London

Contents

This book was created by
Zigzag Publishing Ltd, The Barn,
Randolph's Farm, Brighton Road,
Hurstpierpoint, BN6 9EL, England

Designers: Teresa Foster, Jane Felstead,
 Suzi Hooper, Jenny Searle and
 Jonathan Skelton
Design Manager: Kate Buxton
Additional illustrations: Guy Smith
Consultants: Claire Nozières and
 Katherine Folliot
Pronunciation guide: Philippa Tomlinson
 and Kay Barnham
Series concept: Tony Potter

8320
Color separations by RCS Graphics Ltd, Leeds

Copyright © 1996 Zigzag Publishing Ltd

Published in the United States in 1996 by Courage Books

Printed in Hong Kong

9 8 7 6 5 4 3 2 1
Digit on the right indicates the number of this printing.

ISBN 1 56138 737 1

This book may be ordered by mail from the publisher.
But try your bookstore first!
Published by Courage Books, and imprint of
Running Press Book Publishers
125 South Twenty-second Street
Philadelphia, Pennsylvania 19103-4399

About this book

In this book you can find out all about Spain, Spanish people and the Spanish language. Discover what the Spanish like to eat and drink, what they do for a living and what famous Spanish places look like.

Where Spain is in the world

North America

Europe

Asia

Africa

South America

Australia

Find out what Spanish children do in their spare time and how they celebrate Spanish festivals.

Learn how to speak Spanish from page 26 onwards.

Hello!

¡Hola!

The González family will show you what to say in many situations and how to say these Spanish words. You will find many useful Spanish words and phrases throughout this book to help you increase your Spanish vocabulary.

Map of Spain

Spain is the second largest country in Western Europe. It has borders with France to the north, Portugal to the west, and Gibralter to the south.

The Spanish landscape is very beautiful and varied. There are high mountains in the north and south. The east and south coasts have long sunny beaches. In the center of the country, around Madrid, it is very hot in the summer, but the winters are cold.

Highest mountain: Teide Peak, Tenerife (Canary Islands), 12,198 feet (3,718 meters). This mountain is also an active volcano.

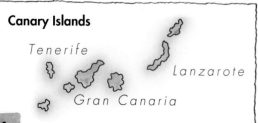

Canary Islands

Tenerife

Lanzarote

Gran Canaria

El Ferrol

La Coruña

Oviedo

Gijón

Asturias

Cantabria

Galicia

Cantabrian Mountains

Vigo

Castile-León

Valladolid

Sego

Salamanca

Sierra de Gredos

Portugal

Tagus

Extremadura

Guadiana

Sierra Morena

Guadalquivir

Córdoba

Seville

Andalusia

Málaga

Torremolinos

el país
country

Cádiz

Marbella

Gibraltar (Br.

Strait of Gibraltar

4

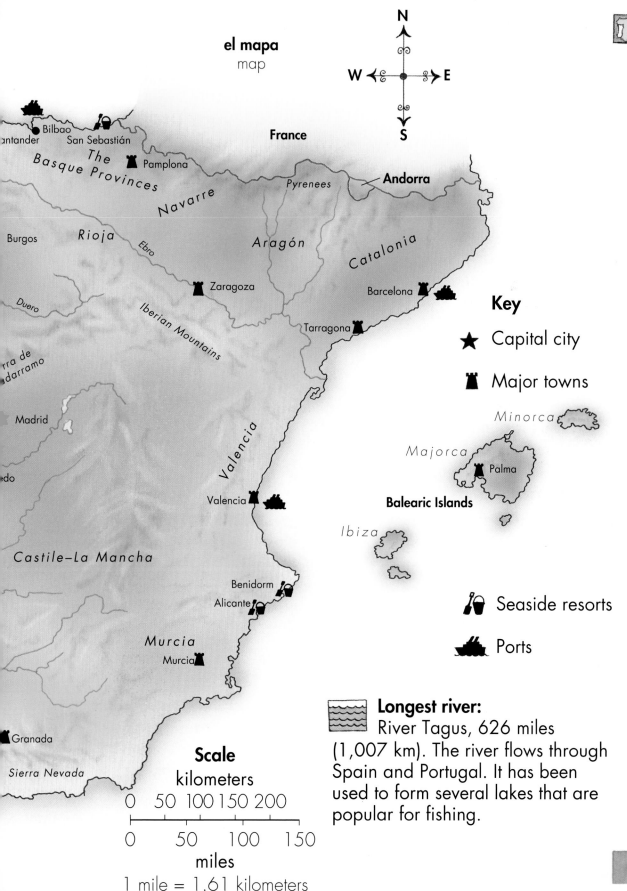

el mapa
map

N

W — E

S

France

Andorra

Santander • Bilbao
San Sebastián

The
Basque Provinces

Pamplona

Navarre

Pyrenees

Burgos

Rioja

Ebro

Aragón

Catalonia

Zaragoza

Barcelona

Duero

Iberian Mountains

Tarragona

Sierra de
Guadarrama

Madrid

Valencia

Key

⭐ Capital city

♟ Major towns

Minorca

Majorca

Palma

Balearic Islands

Valencia

Ibiza

Castile–La Mancha

Benidorm

Alicante

Murcia

Murcia

🪣 Seaside resorts

🚢 Ports

Granada

Scale
kilometers

0   50 100 150 200

Sierra Nevada

0   50   100   150
miles

1 mile = 1.61 kilometers

Longest river:
River Tagus, 626 miles
(1,007 km). The river flows through
Spain and Portugal. It has been
used to form several lakes that are
popular for fishing.

Facts about Spain

Although Spain is about the size of Nevada and Utah together, almost 14 times as many people live there, so it is a much more crowded area.

 Size: 194,896 sq miles (504,783 sq km)

Population: 38,992,000

The Spanish flag looks a bit like a sandwich. It has a slice of red on the top and the bottom, and a yellow stripe in the middle.

In Spain the Head of State is the king. The king does not have much power, though. Important decisions about how the country is run are made by the prime minister and the government.

la bandera
flag

 Official name:
Espãna or **Estado Español** (State of Spain)

 Capital city:
Madrid

Language

Although nearly everyone can speak Spanish (known as **español** or Castilian), other regional languages are still spoken as well. The Spanish are very proud of all their languages.

In Catalonia, a region in the northeast, many people speak Catalan.

el lenguaje
language

Basque is spoken in the region where the north of Spain meets up with the southwest of France, called the Basque Country.

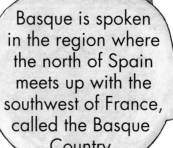

Galician is spoken in Galicia in the northwest.

Money

Spanish money is the **peseta**. A small piece of candy costs about five pesetas.

el dinero
money

There are many different coins and bank notes. Coins are made in amounts of 1, 5, 10, 25, 50, 100, 200, and 500 pesetas.

Peseta notes are made in amounts of 1,000, 2,000, 5,000, and 10,000. Portraits of famous Spanish people are printed on the notes.

On the back of the notes the king's head is shown. Older coins have the head of General Franco, who ruled Spain from 1939 to 1975.

la moneda
coin

el billete de banco
bank note

Some things Spain is well known for

las naranjas
oranges
Valencia
Seville

los artículos de cuero
leather goods

el aceite de oliva
olive oil

el vino
wine
Rioja
Valdepeñas

el jerez
sherry

los coches
cars
Ford Fiesta, Ford Sierra

el turismo
tourism

Regions of Spain

Spain is divided into many regions. These include the Balearic Islands in the Mediterranean Sea, and the Canary Islands in the Atlantic Ocean, near the coast of Africa.

The Basque region in the north is sometimes called Green Spain as a lot of rain falls here all year round, making the land very fertile.

The northwest coast of Galicia is dotted with craggy inlets and old fishing villages.

San Sebastián and Santander are elegant seaside resorts on the north coast.

The center of Spain is boiling hot in the summer, but freezing cold in the winter.

Further south, the weather gets hotter and hotter and the land more and more dry.

Thousands of tourists from all over Europe spend their vacations at seaside resorts on the east coast. Benidorm on the Costa Blanca is one of the busiest.

el centro de turismo
resort

la casa
house

Further south along the east coast, orange groves surround the old city of Valencia. Among the groves are the farmers' small white-washed houses.

Rice is also grown in this region. Water from nearby rivers is used to flood the huge rice fields. With Valencia's warm climate, the rice grows quickly in the artificial lakes.

The southern region of Andalusia is the hottest and driest part of all Europe. On the coast, the Costa del Sol is very popular with vacationers. Wine is produced inland.

Some buildings in Andalusia look North African. This is because Spain was ruled by Arabs from North Africa for about 800 years.

Although Andalusia is very hot, the slopes of the Sierra Nevada are so high that people can ski there in winter.

Wild boar, wild goats, eagles, and vultures live in the mountains of the Pyrenees and southern Spain.

el ave
bird

The Canary Islands are covered with volcanoes. On the island of Lanzarote, the rocky landscape is very dramatic. Grapevines grow well in the black earth.

There are many national parks in Spain. Rare animals such as the Iberian mongoose and the Mediterranean lynx can be found to the south of Seville.

el animal
animal

Madrid

Madrid is Spain's capital city. It is situated in the middle of the country. More than three and a half million people live there.

Although the center of the city still has its old buildings, the outskirts are now crowded with huge modern blocks of apartments.

There are many squares in Madrid. The main one is called the **Plaza Mayor**. People wander through here, or sit in the sun at one of the cafés. It is also used for plays and pageants.

One of the most important buildings in Madrid is **El Museo del Prado**, an art gallery that contains many beautiful paintings.

Another big square is the **Plaza de España**. In the middle there is a statue of Don Quixote and Sancho Panza. The Spanish writer Cervantes, who invented these characters, died in Madrid in 1616.

Retiro Park was built by King Philip II. It has fountains, rose gardens, and a huge lake for boating.

Some famous sites

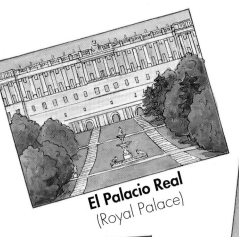
El Palacio Real
(Royal Palace)

Cibeles Fountain

La Puerta del Sol
(This is the center of the old city. There is a statue of a bear and a tree, which are the symbols of Madrid.)

Church of San Jerónimo
(where royal marriages take place)

La Puerta de Alcalá
(one of the city's gates)

Plaza Mayor
(main square in Madrid)

Gran Vía
(major shopping street)

In a typical Spanish town

Most Spanish towns and villages are built around a square (la plaza). Here, people meet and sit in the sun.

As well as supermarkets, all Spanish towns have a market area where you can buy every sort of fresh food. They are busy places, full of life and noise.

la pastelería
pastry shop

la oficina de turismo
tourist office

el estanco
tobacconist

la panadería
bakery

el ayuntamiento
town hall

el banco
bank

la tienda de ultramarinos
grocery store

la ferretería
hardware store

la policía
police officer

Most people live in apartments. The furniture is often made of dark, polished wood. The Spanish like to have wooden or tiled floors to help keep their homes cool in the summer.

The church is an important part of every town. On Sundays, many families dress up and go to Mass in the morning.

Children often meet and play together in the town's square. In the evening, many families go out walking together. This is called **el paseo**.

la iglesia
church

la farmacia
pharmacy

el supermercado
supermarket

la papelería
stationers

la oficina de correos
post office

el quiosco
newspaper stand

Eating in Spain

The Spanish enjoy their food and they often eat out. At meals, family and friends can meet and talk about the day's events.

Breakfast (**el desayuno**) is very simple. Children might have a glass of warm milk and some cake or toast.

Halfway through the morning, people eat a sandwich or roll (**el bocadillo**).

Some typical Spanish Dishes

Spain is famous for its **paella**. This is a colorful dish made with rice, saffron, and many types of seafood, such as lobster, shrimp, and mussels.

el gazpacho
tomato soup

los calamares
squid

la tortilla de patatas
omelette with potatoes

la fabada
thick bean and meat soup

Drink

el vino
wine
(Cava, Rioja, Valdepeñas)

el jerez
sherry

la sangría
(made with red wine,
lemon and orange juice,
brandy, lemonade, and ice)

Bread is eaten with every meal.
The main meal (**la comida**) is
eaten between 2 P.M. and 3 P.M.
The first course might be cold
tomato soup (**el gazpacho**), a
salad, or vegetables. Fish or
meat and French fries or salad
are eaten as a second course.

la cerveza
beer
(San Miguel)

la horchata
(made from milk
and almonds)

> For dessert, the
> Spanish like fresh fruit,
> custard (**flan**),
> or ice cream.

el blanco y negro
(coffee with vanilla
ice cream on top)

el granzado
(fruit drink)

la mortadela
slices of meat
with olives

las tapas
tiny portions of food,
appetizers

el flan
custard

la tarta de manzana
apple pie

el chorizo
spicy sausage

What people do

Although there are many big industrial towns, much of Spain is still covered in countryside. Spain produces more food than many other European countries.

Olives are an important crop. They are grown all over Spain, except in the northwest. Spain exports more olive oil than any other country in the world.

la oveja
sheep

The merino sheep is raised in many parts of Spain. Its curly, silky fleece makes fine wool. Goats are grazed on the poorer land.

el granjero
farmer

The automobile industry employs more people in Spain than any other industry. Spain sells more cars abroad than any other west European country.

Farmers also grow wheat, barley, and rice. Oranges and tomatoes from the south and east are sold abroad. They bring a lot of money into the country.

el coche
car

Many people work in the fishing industry. Spain has the third largest fishing fleet in Europe. Fish is eaten all over the country, especially in Galicia.

el pescador
fisherman

16

Coal, lead, copper, zinc, and mercury are mined. The mines employ many people.

la fábrica
factory

Since the 1950s, Spain has become more and more industrialized. Large numbers of people have moved into the towns to look for work.

Many Spanish people work in factories that make things such as clothes, shoes, and other leather goods, cars, ceramics, chemicals, and computers.

Spain has more vineyards than anywhere else in the world. Wine and sherry are produced and sold all over the world.

la uva
grape

Bananas and grapes for wine are major crops on the Canary Islands. They are exported to other countries.

el plátano
banana

Even more people, though, work in the tourist industry. They work in bars and cafés, and in the huge hotels that have been built for vacationers along the sunny eastern and southern coasts.

Children in Spain

Here you can find out something about school days in Spain, and about how Spanish children spend their time.

 School in Spain starts early in the morning, and finishes around 5 P.M. There is a long break between 1 P.M. and 3 P.M. for lunch. Most children go home for this.

All Spanish children between the ages of 6 and 16 must go to school. After this, they can either leave and look for a job, or continue studying.

Most children go to schools that are free, run by the government. Other children go to private schools run by the Catholic Church, which the parents must pay for.

la escuela
school

los vestidos
clothes

Spanish children do not normally have to wear a uniform, so they can wear their own clothes to school.

We have two or three weeks of vacation at Christmas and one week at Easter.

We have 2½ months off from school in the summer.

In June, the schools shut at lunchtime because it is too hot in the afternoon to have classes.

During the school vacations, Spanish children spend a lot of time outside. They might go to meet their friends at a nearby swimming pool, or play soccer together.

el fútbol
soccer

la piscina
swimming pool

Spanish children are allowed to stay up to watch television or play with their friends until very late. It is often after midnight when they go to bed.

Most Spanish families still spend their vacations in Spain. In the summer, they may go to the seaside, or to the mountains to escape from the heat. In the winter, they may go skiing in the mountains.

las vacaciones
vacations

During festivals, children dress up in the traditional costumes of their region. Many Spanish children learn **flamenco** dancing.

esquiar
skiing

los niños
children

History of Spain

Two thousand years ago Spain, like most of Europe, was part of the huge Roman Empire. These are some of the major events that have taken place since then:

A.D. 711

Muslim Arabs from the north of Africa invaded Spain. They took control of the country and ruled for almost 800 years. They built beautiful palaces such as the Alhambra in Granada.

1479

Ferdinand, the King of Spain, and his wife, Queen Isabella, set out to unite Spain against the Arabs.

1492

Finally, Ferdinand and Isabella's armies defeated the Arabs in Granada. The Arabs no longer had any power in Spain.

In the same year, Christopher Columbus discovered America for Ferdinand and Isabella. Spain began to colonize the New World. It also ruled the Netherlands and parts of Belgium and Italy. As a result, it became the richest and most powerful country in Europe.

el buque
ship

1588

Philip II of Spain tried to conquer England with a huge fleet of ships. His Spanish Armada was defeated, however, by Elizabeth I's forces.

Spain was invaded by the French Emperor, Napoleon, who put his brother on the Spanish throne. The Spanish fought back, however, and the French were expelled.

The King of Spain was overthrown by the republicans and a new government was set up. This led to the Spanish Civil War.

In 1936, a Spanish general, Francisco Franco, rebelled against the republican government. Civil War broke out between his troops and supporters of the government.

One million Spaniards were killed in the Spanish Civil War. Franco won and went on to rule Spain as a dictator until 1975. Under his rule, Spain remained poor and cut off from the rest of Europe.

Now

Today democracy has been restored and Spain is a prosperous modern country. In 1986 it joined the European Economic Community.

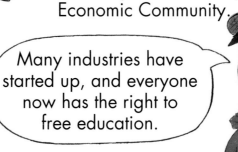

Many industries have started up, and everyone now has the right to free education.

21

Famous places

Every year, about 42 million tourists visit Spain. Many people from Britain, Germany, the Netherlands, and Scandinavia like to take their vacations along the hot and sunny Spanish coast.

Two of the most popular seaside resorts are Benidorm and Torremolinos on the Mediterranean coast. Benidorm was once a small fishing village. Today it is vast. Tall blocks of vacation apartments line the beaches, surrounded by bars, cafés, and discos.

> Most tourists visit Spain for the sea and sun, but there are many old and beautiful parts of the country to visit inland.

la playa
beach

The coastline of the beautiful Balearic Islands has interesting caves to explore, as well as sandy beaches that are perfect for swimming and sunbathing.

In the southern city of Granada is the palace of the Alhambra. It was built in the Arab style in the thirteenth and fourteenth centuries. The palace gardens are full of lakes and fountains.

One of the most famous buildings in Seville is the Giralda. This is a tower also built by the Arabs from north Africa (who were Muslims). Today it is part of Seville Cathedral.

la catedral
cathedral

22

el palacio
palace

Near Madrid is the ancient town of Toledo. Its ancient spired cathedral contains many paintings by the famous artist El Greco.

The artist, Picasso, lived in Barcelona for a time, and many of his paintings are kept there.

la pintura
painting

The royal palace of El Escorial is just outside Madrid. It is a huge stone building. It looks a bit like a castle from a frightening fairy tale. Inside are the graves of many of Spain's kings, queens, princes, and princesses.

In Barcelona, the strange buildings of the architect Gaudí can be found. The **Sagrada Familia** (Holy Family) church, which Gaudí never finished, is sometimes called the Sandcastle Cathedral.

The ancient aqueduct of Segovia was built by the Romans in the first century A.D. It brought water from the Sierra Fonfría, 8 miles (14 km) away.

Summer is not the only season that is good for tourism. Many tourists enjoy the mild weather on the coast in the winter. Some go to the ski resorts in the mountains of the Sierra Nevada and the Pyrenees.

23

Festivals

Spanish holidays (fiestas) are a spectacular mixture of color, music, parades, costumes, and dancing. They take place throughout the year to celebrate various religious events. They might also be held to celebrate the beginning of spring, or the autumn harvest.

Romerías are picnic outings to a saint's shrine, held in country districts. People travel on horseback or in white covered wagons decorated with flowers. They sing and play guitars and castanets.

One of the most important fiestas is held in Seville during **Semana Santa** (Holy Week, the week before Easter). The people dress up in costumes decorated with semi-precious stones. Crucifixes and holy statues are carried on floats while sorrowful hymns are sung.

Seville's **Feria de abril** (April festival) is even noisier and more colorful than **Semana Santa**. Far into the night people sing and dance to **flamenco** music. Guitars and castanets are played. Many people wear traditional gypsy costumes.

el bailador
dancer

On the second Thursday after Whitsun, the festival of Corpus Christi is celebrated throughout Spain. The streets are covered in flowers, the town bells are rung, and there are noisy firework displays.

24

el modelo
model

In March, Valencia celebrates the **Fallas de San José**. Artists spend all year making huge paper-mâché models of people. These are painted with fantastic colors and put up in the squares or plazas all around the city.

los fuegos artificiales
fireworks

On the last night, the figures are burned on huge bonfires and fireworks are set off. The fire brigade has to make sure that the people and the nearby buildings are safe.

Many of Spain's festivals include bullfights. In some fiestas, the bulls run through the streets.

el toro
bull

At the San Fermín festival in the northern city of Pamplona, the people run with the bulls, trying to distract them with rolled-up newspapers.

25

How to speak Spanish

Now you can find out how to speak Spanish.
The González family show you what to say in many different
situations. Here they are to introduce themselves.

The González family

¡Hola! Somos el Señor y la Señora González.
(Olla! Somoss el Senyor ee la Senyora Gonzalez.)
Hello! We are Señor and Señora González.

¡Hola! Soy Miguel.
(Olla! Soy Miggel.)
Hello! I'm Miguel.

¡Hola! Soy Carmen.
(Olla! Soy Carmen.)
Hello! I'm Carmen.

Everything the González family says is written in both Spanish
and English. There is also a guide to help you pronounce
the Spanish words.

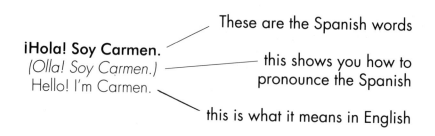

¡Hola! Soy Carmen.
(Olla! Soy Carmen.)
Hello! I'm Carmen.

These are the Spanish words

this shows you how to
pronounce the Spanish

this is what it means in English

How to say Spanish words

These notes will help you to use the pronunciation guide:

Say 'a' like the 'a' in 'bad'.   Say 'o' like the 'o' in 'top'.
Say 'e' like the 'e' in 'bed'.   Say 'oo' like the 'oo' in 'good'.
Say 'ay' like the 'ay' in 'say'.   Say 'ch' like the 'ch' in 'church'.
Say 'ee' like the 'ee' in 'feet'.   Say 'cee' like the word 'see'.

- 'B' is used for the Spanish 'v'.
- 'Ny' is used in the guide to make the sound of the Spanish 'ñ'.
- 'H' is used for the Spanish 'j' and is pronounced like the 'h' in 'hole'.

¿Question marks?

When there is a question or exclamation mark at the end of a sentence, the Spanish also put an upside-down question or exclamation mark at the beginning of the sentence.

Speaking to people

When you speak to a close friend or a relative, you use **tú**. If there is more than one friend or relative, you use **vosotros** (or **vosotras** if the group is female only). When you speak to somebody you do not know very well, you use **usted**. If there is more than one person you use **ustedes**.

Accents

In general, the second to last syllable of a Spanish word is stressed. When a different syllable is stressed, it is marked by an accent.

Masculine and feminine words

In Spanish, some words are masculine and some are feminine. **La** in front of a word means that it is is feminine and **el** usually means that it is masculine. For example, 'house' is feminine in Spanish - '**la** casa', while 'book' is masculine - '**el** libro'.

When the word is plural, for example, books or houses, then it has **las** or **los** in front of it ('**las** casas' and '**los** libros'). **Las** is the feminine plural and **los** is the masculine plural.

Meeting people

In the evenings, the González family often goes to the town center for a walk. When Hispanic people meet somebody that they do not know very well, they use the polite form of Spanish. Children also use this polite form when they speak to people older than themselves.

To say 'How are you?' in polite Spanish you can use '¿Cómo está?'. If you are speaking to more than one person you can say '¿Cómo están?'.

Buenas noches, Señor Sánchez. ¿Cómo está?
(Bwennas nochess, Senyor Sanchez. Como esta?)
Good evening, Señor Sanchez. How are you?

Muy bien, gracias.
(Mwee bee-en, grasyas.)
Very well, thank you.

When you meet somebody you know well, you can say '¿Cómo estás?'. If you are talking to more than one friend you can say '¿Cómo estáis?'.

¡Hola! ¿Cómo estás?
(Olla! Como estas?)
Hello! How are you?

Bien, gracias.
(Bee-en, grasyas.)
Fine, thank you.

28

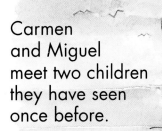

Carmen and Miguel meet two children they have seen once before.

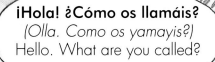

¡Hola! ¿Cómo os llamáis?
(Olla. Como os yamayis?)
Hello. What are you called?

Me llamo Francisco.
(May yamo Frasisco.)
I'm called Francisco.

Nos llamamos Carmen y Miguel.
(Nos yamamos Carmen ee Miggel.)
We're called Carmen and Miguel.

Tengo diez años.
(Tengo deeyez anyos.)
I'm ten years old.

¡Vámonos! ¡Hasta luego!
(Bamonos! Asta lwego!)
Let's go! See you later!

¿Nos vemos aquí mañana?
(Nos bemos akee manyanna?)
Shall we meet here tomorrow?

¡Yo también!
(Yo tambee-en!)
Me too!

De acuerdo. Hasta mañana.
(Day akwerdo. Asta manyanna.)
OK. See you tomorrow.

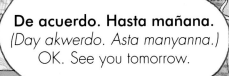

Meeting people words

buenas tardes
(bwennas tardes)
good afternoon/
good evening

buenos días
(bwennos dee-as)
good morning

adiós
(addyoss)
goodbye

¿y tú?
(ee too?)
and you?

bastante bien
(bastantay bee-en)
quite well

Making friends

On their way home from school, Carmen and Miguel talk to an English boy and girl who started at their school that day. They talk about their families and where they live.

¡Hola Ann!
Esta es mi hermana, Carmen.
(Olla Ann! Esta ess mee ermana, Carmen.)
Hello Ann! This is my sister, Carmen.

¡Soy John,
el hermano de Ann!
(Soy John, el ermano day Ann!)
I'm John, Ann's brother!

¡Hola!
(Olla!)
Hello!

¿De dónde sois?
(Day donday soyis?)
Where are you from?

Ahora vivimos en España.
(A-ora bibeemos en Espanya.)
We live in Spain now.

Somos de Inglaterra.
(Somoss day Inglaterra.)
We're from England.

¿Vivís en esta calle?
(Bibeess en esta kaiyay?)
Do you live in this street?

Mi hermano no habla
español muy bien.
*(Mee ermano no abla
espanyol mwee bee-en.)*
My brother doesn't speak
much Spanish.

Lo siento. No entiendo.
(Lo seeyento. No entyendo.)
I'm sorry. I don't understand.

Family words

la familia
(la fameelya)
family

los padres
(los padress)
parents

el padre
(el padray)
father

el abuelo
(el abwelo)
grandfather

el tío
(el tee-o)
uncle

la tía
(la tee-a)
aunt

la madre
(la madray)
mother

la abuela
(la abwela)
grandmother

la hermana
(la ermana)
sister

el hermano
(el ermano)
brother

el primo
(el preemo)
cousin (male)

la prima
(la preema)
cousin (female)

el hijo
(el i-ho)
son

la hija
(la i-ha)
daughter

Finding the way

Señora González has taken her children out for the day. Before they go home they decide to have something to eat at a nearby café.

Por favor señora, ¿hay un café por aquí?
(Por fabbor senyora, eye oon caffay por akee?)
Excuse me madam, is there a café near here?

¿Está lejos?
(Esta layhos?)
Is it far?

No.
(No.)
No.

Por allí y gire a la izquierda.
(Por ayee ee heeray ah la izkeeyerda.)
Over there and turn left.

la cabina telefónica
(la cabeena telefonnika)
telephone booth

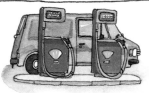

la gasolinera
(la gasolinerra)
gas station

los servicios
(los serbeeceeyos)
toilets

el buzón
(el boozon)
mailbox

Direction words

todo recto
(toddo recto)
straight on

frente a
(frentay ah)
opposite

al lado de
(al laddo day)
next to

a la derecha
(ah la deretcha)
on the right

a la izquierda
(ah la izkeeyerda)
on the left

After their meal, they ask a man the way to the station.

On the way home, Carmen gets lost. Her mother tries to find her.

¿Dónde está la estación, por favor?
(Donday esta la estacyon, por fabbor?)
Where is the station, please?

Me he perdido.
(May ay perdeedo.)
I am lost.

¡No encuentro a mí hija!
(No encwentro ah mee i-ha!)
I can't find my daughter!

Está a la derecha.
(Esta ah la deretcha.)
It's on the right.

el aeropuerto
(el aeropwerto)
airport

el hospital
(el ospital)
hospital

la comisaría
(la comisareeya)
police station

sobre
(sobray)
on

en
(en)
in

hasta
(asta)
as far as

cerca de aquí
(serka day akee)
nearby

en coche
(en cochay)
by car

a pie
(ah peeyay)
on foot

la iglesia
(la iglessya)
church

Staying in a hotel or house

The Spanish often have the whole month of August as holiday. During this month the González family likes to go to different parts of Spain. This year they are staying in a hotel for the first week, and in a friend's house for the second.

Nos gustaría reservar una habitación para una semana.
(Nos goostareeya reserbar oona abitaceeyon parra oona semanna.)
We would like to book a room for one week.

Sí señores. ¿Qué desean ustedes?
(See senyores. Kay desayan oostedes?)
Yes, sir and madam. What would you like?

Una habitación doble con baño, por favor.
(Oona abitaceeyon dobblay con banyo, por fabbor.)
A double room with a bathroom, please.

¡Me gusta este hotel!
(May goosta estay otel!)
I like this hotel!

la almohada
(la almwadda)
pillow

la sábana
(la sabbanna)
sheet

el mozo
(el mozo)
porter

el balcón
(el balkon)
balcony

la cama
(la camma)
bed

la casa
(la casa)
house

arriba
(areeba)
upstairs

el dormitorio
(el dormitorreeyo)
bedroom

el cuarto de baño
(el cwarto day banyo)
bathroom

la butaca
(la bootacca)
armchair

la sala de estar
(la salla day estar)
living room

el televisor
(el telebissor)
television set

el comedor
(el commedor)
dining room

la puerta
(la pwerta)
door

la cocina
(la coseena)
kitchen

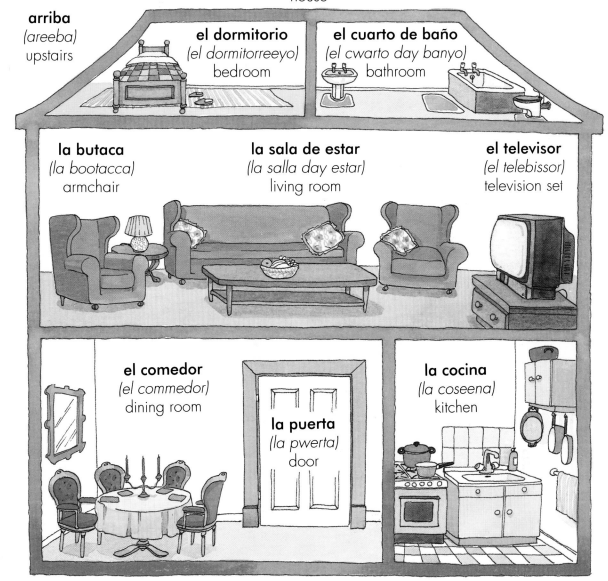

las contraventanas
(las contrabentannas)
shutters

la ventana
(la bentanna)
window

la mesa
(la messa)
table

la silla
(la seeya)
chair

Camping

The González family is spending the last week of August on a campsite. Most Spanish campsites provide electricity, so that the campers can watch television or enjoy themselves as they would at home.

Por favor, ¿se puede acampar aquí?
(Por fabbor, say pwedday acampar akee?)
Excuse me, may we camp here?

Tenemos dos tiendas y un remolque.
(Tenemos doss teeyendas ee oon remolkay.)
We have two tents and a camper.

Nos gustaría quedarnos siete días.
(Nos goostareeya keddarnos syettay dee-as.)
We'd like to stay for seven days.

Sí, de acuerdo.
(See, day akwerdo.)
Yes, that's fine.

¿Dónde está la tienda del camping?
(Donday esta la teeyenda del camping?)
Where is the campsite shop?

Está por allá.
(Esta por ayah.)
It's over there.

Por favor, ¿pueden hacer un poco menos de ruido?
(Por fabbor, pwedden aser oon poco mennos day rooeedo?)
Please could you make a little less noise?

Some more useful camping words and phrases

agua potable
(agwa potahblay)
drinking water

reservado para remolques
(reserbahdo parra remolkays)
recreational vehicles only

agua no potable
(agwa no potahblay)
non-drinking water

la tela impermeable
(la tella impermayabblay)
groundsheet

el camping
(el camping)
campsite

la tienda de campaña
(la teeyenda day campanya)
tent

el palo de la tienda
(el pallo day la teeyenda)
tent pole

el camping gas
(el camping gas)
camping gas

la estaca de la tienda
(la estacca day la teeyenda)
tent peg

el saco de dormir
(el sacco day dormeer)
sleeping bag

las duchas
(las doochas)
showers

el mazo
(el maso)
mallet

el colchón neumático
(el colchon newmattico)
airbed

¿Dónde están los servicios, por favor?
(Donday estan los serbeeceeyos, por fabbor?)
Where are the toilets, please?

Lo siento, ni idea.
(Lo seeyento, nee iday-ah.)
I'm sorry, I've no idea.

Están al lado de la tienda del camping.
(Estan al laddo day la teeyenda del camping.)
They are next to the campsite shop.

Going shopping

In most parts of Spain, the shops are open from 9 in the morning until 2 in the afternoon. They open again at 5 and close for the day at 8 in the evening.

¿Puedo ayudarle?
(Pweddo ayoodahlay?)
Can I help you?

Querría dos panes, por favor.
(Kerreeya doss pannes, por fabbor.)
I would like two loaves, please.

Food words

la leche
(la lechay)
milk

la mantequilla
(la mantekeeya)
butter

el yogurt
(el yogoort)
yoghurt

el huevo
(el webo)
egg

la patata
(la patatta)
potato

la col
(la coll)
cabbage

el tomate
(el tomattay)
tomato

la naranja
(la naranha)
orange

la manzana
(la manzanna)
apple

la carne
(la carnay)
meat

el pollo
(el pollo)
chicken

el azúcar
(el asoocar)
sugar

la mermelada
(la mermeladda)
jam

la carnicería
(la carnisereeya)
butcher's shop

el supermercado
(el supermercaddo)
supermarket

la panadería
(la pannadereeya)
bakery

Although the Spanish like to go to their local shops, supermarkets are being used more and more.

¿Desea algo más?
(Desaya algo mass?)
Would you like anything else?

¿Cuánto es?
(Cwanto ess?)
How much is it?

Dos mil pesetas.
(Doss meel pessettas.)
Two thousand pesetas.

Un kilo de tomates, por favor.
(Oon keelo day tomattess, por fabbor.)
A kilo of tomatoes, please.

la farmacia
(la farmaceeya)
pharmacy

la librería
(la librereeya)
bookshop

la tienda de ultramarinos
(la teeyenda day ultramareenos)
grocery shop

The post office and bank

Carmen and Miguel are at their local post office (correos y telégrafos).

¿Cuánto cuesta enviar este paquete?
(Cwanto cwesta enbeeyar estay pakettay?)
How much is it to send this parcel?

¿A dónde?
(Ah donday?)
Where to?

A Inglaterra.
(Ah Inglaterra.)
To England.

If you want to post letters abroad, look for a letter-box marked 'extranjero'.

Now Carmen is telephoning a friend. When the Spanish answer the telephone they say 'dígame'.

¡Dígame! ¿Quién habla?
(Deegamay! Keeyen abla?)
Hello! Who's speaking?

Soy Carmen. ¿Puedo hablar con Teresa, por favor?
(Soy Carmen. Pweddo ablah con Teressa por fabbor?)
It's Carmen. May I speak to Teresa please?

el dinero
(el dinerro)
money

el banco
(el banco)
bank

la moneda
(la monedda)
coin

la carta
(la carta)
letter

la tarjeta postal
(la tarhetta postal)
postcard

Post office and bank words

correos y telégrafos
(corrayos ee telaygrafos)
post office

por avión
(por abyon)
airmail

número de teléfono
(noomerro day telayfono)
telephone number

Te llamo más tarde.
(Tay yammo mass tarday.)
I'll call you back later.

enviar
(enbeeyar)
to send

extranjero
(extranherro)
foreign

el tipo de cambio
(el teepo day cambyo)
exchange rate

Señor González has gone to the bank to change some Spanish pesetas into English pounds and pence.

¿A cuánto está la libra?
(Ah cwanto esta la leebra?)
How many pesetas are there to the pound?

el sello
(el seyo)
stamp

el billete
(el beeyettay)
note

el paquete
(el pakettay)
parcel

el teléfono
(el telayfono)
telephone

la tarjeta de crédito
(la tarhetta day creditto)
credit card

41

Eating out

The González family often has Sunday lunch at a friendly local restaurant.

Un vaso de vino tinto, por favor.
(Oon basso day beeno tinto, por fabbor.)
A glass of red wine, please.

Quiero una limonada.
(Keeyerro oona limmonadda.)
I'd like a lemonade.

¿Qué más desean?
(Kay mass dessayan?)
What else would you like?

Un agua mineral, por favor.
(Oon agwa minneral, por fabbor.)
Mineral water, please.

¿Te gusta el helado de fresa?
(Tay goosta el elahdo day fraysa?)
Do you like strawberry ice cream?

No, prefiero el helado de chocolate.
(No, prefeeayro el elahdo day chocolatay.)
No, I prefer chocolate ice cream.

el vaso
(el basso)
glass

el menú
(el menoo)
menu

la ensalada
(la ensaladda)
salad

el filete
(el filettay)
steak

las patatas fritas
(las patattas freetass)
French fries

42

el pescado
(el peskaddo)
fish

la paella
(la pie-ayah)
paella

el camarero
(el cammarerro)
waiter

La cuenta, por favor.
(La cwenta, por fabbor.)
The bill, please.

¡Aquí lo tiene!
(Akee lo teeyennay!)
Here it is!

¡Buen provecho!
(Bwen probbecho!)
Enjoy your meal!

¿Está bueno?
(Esta bwenno?)
Is it good?

Sí. Está muy rico.
(See. Esta mwee reeko.)
Yes. It's very tasty.

¿Me puedes pasar la sal?
(May pweddess passar la sal?)
Could you pass me the salt?

¡Tengo hambre!
(Tengo ambray!)
I'm hungry!

¡Tengo sed!
(Tengo sed!)
I'm thirsty!

la tortilla de patatas
(la torteeya day patattas)
Spanish omelette

una taza de café
(oona taza day caffay)
a cup of coffee

una jarra de agua
(oona harra day agwa)
a jug of water

43

Visiting places

Spain is famous for its sunshine and sandy beaches. As well as going to the seaside, the González family also likes to visit old Spanish castles and small white-washed villages.

¿Es antiguo aquel castillo?
(Ess anteegwo akel casteeyo?)
Is that castle old?

Sí. Es muy antiguo.
(See. Ess mwee anteegwo.)
Yes. It's very old.

Useful visiting words

el partido de fútbol
(el parteedo day footbol)
soccer match

el parque de atracciones
(el parkay day attrakseeyonness)
fairground

el centro turístico
(el thentro turistico)
tourist center

el palacio
(el palathee-o)
palace

el castillo
(el casteeyo)
castle

la película
(la paylikoola)
film

las cuevas
(las cwebbas)
caves

el teatro
(el tayattro)
theater

el circo
(el seerko)
circus

la obra de teatro
(la obbra day tayattro)
play

el museo
(el moossayo)
museum

el cine
(el seenay)
cinema

¡Qué bonito es este pueblo!
(Kay boneeto ess estay pweblo!)
This village is pretty!

45

Games and sports

la gimnasia
(la gymnassiya)
gymnastics

el fútbol
(el footbol)
soccer

el patinaje
(el patteenahay)
skating

la natación
(la nattaceeyon)
swimming

el cricket
(el cricket)
cricket

la equitación
(la ekeetaceeyon)
riding

el windsurf
(el windsoorf)
windsurfing

Carmen and Miguel have met up with some of their friends in the local park.

¿A qué estáis jugando?
(Ah kay estayiss hoogando?)
What are you playing?

A béisbol.
(Ah basebol.)
Baseball.

¿Cómo se juega? ¿Es difícil?
(Como say hwegga? Ess difeeseel?)
How do you play? Is it difficult?

No. Es fácil.
(No. Ess faseel.)
No. It's easy.

¿Me dejáis jugar?
(May dayhayiss hoogar?)
Can I play?

¡Claro! Necesitamos dieciocho personas.
(Klaroh! Nesesitamos deeyeseeocho personas.)
Of course! We need eighteen people.

el juego del escondite
(el hweggo del eskondeetay)
hide and seek

el ping-pong
(el ping-pong)
ping-pong

la pesca
(la peska)
fishing

practicar el remo
(practicah el remo)
rowing

el ciclismo
(el seekleesmo)
cycling

el judo
(el hoodo)
judo

¿Dónde está la pelota?
(Donday esta la pelota?)
Where is the ball?

¡Está aquí!
(Esta akee!)
It's here!

¡Te toca a ti!
(Tay tocca ah tee!)
Your turn!

el poste
(el postay)
post

¡Tengo sueño!
(Tengo swenyo!)
I'm tired!

el palo
(el pallo)
bat

el esquí
(el eskee)
skiing

el footing
(el footing)
jogging

el golf
(el golf)
golf

el baloncesto
(el balonsesto)
basketball

el tenis
(el tennis)
tennis

Accidents and illnesses

The González family keeps all its emergency telephone numbers near the telephone. In Spain there are different numbers for police, ambulance and fire emergencies.

¡Socorro!
(Socorro!)
Help!

¡Fuego!
(Fweggo!)
Fire!

Accident words

¡Cuidado!
(Cweedaddo!)
Watch out!

el coche de la policía
(el cochay day la poliseeya)
police car

la urgencia
(la urgenseeya)
emergency

¡Han entrado a robar en mi habitación!
(An entraddo ah robah en mee abitaceeyon!)
My room has been burgled!

la herida
(la ereeda)
injury

¡Me han robado el bolso!
(May an robaddo el bolso!)
My handbag has been stolen!

la ambulancia
(la ambulanseeya)
ambulance

¡Vengan pronto!
(Bengan pronto!)
Come quickly!

¡Me han robado el billetero!
(May an robaddo el beeyeterro!)
My wallet has been stolen!

48

Illness words

Tengo una erupción.
(Tengo oona erroopceeyon.)
I have a rash.

la tirita
(la tireeta)
adhesive bandage

¡Tengo fiebre!
(Tengo feeyebbray!)
I have a temperature!

Tengo dolor de muelas.
(Tengo dollor day mwellas.)
I have a toothache.

el dentista
(el denteesta)
dentist

Tengo algo en el ojo.
(Tengo algo en el o-ho.)
I have something in my eye.

Travelling

The González family is driving to the railway station. They are all meeting some friends from Madrid.

On the way, the family stops the car for some more gas.

¿Dónde está la estación de servicio más cercana?
(Donday esta la estaceeyon day serbeeceeyo mass thercanna?)
Where is the nearest gas station?

Todo recto.
(Toddo recto.)
Straight on.

 la taquilla
(la takeeya)
ticket office

 la consigna
(la consin ya)
left luggage office

la sala de espera
(la salla day esperra)
waiting room

¿Dónde está la taquilla?
(Donday esta la takeeya?)
Where is the ticket office?

¿A qué hora llega el tren de Madrid?
(Ah kay orra yega el tren day Madrid?)
At what time does the train from Madrid arrive?

A las once.
(Ah las onsay.)
At eleven o'clock.

Detrás de usted.
(Detras day oosted.)
Behind you.

You can find out more about how to say the time in Spanish by looking at page 52.

Later, the friends go
into the town center
by themselves.

¿Dónde está la parada del autobús
para el centro ciudad?
*(Donday esta la paradda del owtobooss
parra el sentro ceeoodad?)*
Where is the bus stop
for the town center?

Está aquí.
(Esta akee.)
It's here.

bajarse
(baharsay)
to get off

el pasajero
(el passaherro)
passenger

subirse
(soobeersay)
to get on

Travelling words

coger el autobús
(cohair el owtobooss)
to catch the bus

el billete de ida y vuelta
(el beeyettay day eeda ee bwelta)
return ticket

el billete
(el beeyettay)
ticket

el mapa
(el mappa)
map

el camión
(el camyon)
truck

dirección única
(dirrekceeyon oonika)
one way

la calle
(la kaiyay)
street

el coche
(el cochay)
car

coger el tren
(cohair el tren)
to catch the train

reservar un asiento
(reserbar oon asseeyento)
to reserve a seat

el autocar
(el owtocar)
coach

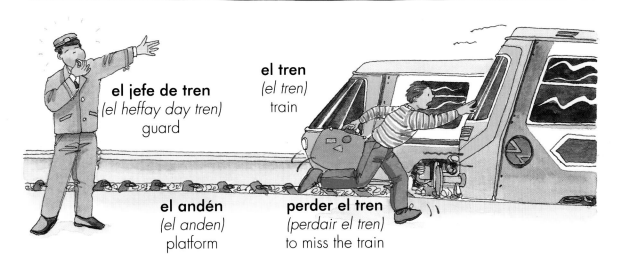

el jefe de tren
(el heffay day tren)
guard

el tren
(el tren)
train

el andén
(el anden)
platform

perder el tren
(perdair el tren)
to miss the train

More useful words

Time

The Spanish do not use the words 'past' or 'to' when they tell the time. Instead, they use the words 'and' (y), or 'less' (menos).

¿Qué hora es, por favor?
(Kay orra ess, por fabbor?)
What time is it, please?

Son las cinco.
(Son las ceenko.)
It is five o'clock.

Son las cinco y diez.
(Son las ceenko ee deeyez.)
It is ten past five.

Son las cinco y cuarto.
(Son las ceenko ee cwarto.)
It is quarter past five.

Son las cinco y media.
(Son las ceenko ee medya.)
It is half past five.

Son las seis menos cuarto.
(Son las seys mennos cwarto.)
It is quarter to six.

Es mediodía.
(Ess medyodee-a.)
It is midday.

Es medianoche.
(Ess medyanochay.)
It is midnight.

Times of the day

la tarde
(la tarday)
afternoon

la noche
(la nochay)
night

la mañana
(la manyanna)
morning

la tarde
(la tarday)
evening (early)

la noche
(la nochay)
evening (late)

enero
(enerro)
January

febrero
(febrerro)
February

marzo
(marzo)
March

abril
(abreel)
April

mayo
(mayo)
May

junio
(hooneeyo)
June

The months of the year and days of the week

The Spanish do not use capital letters at the beginning of the names of the months or the days of the week.

lunes *(looness)* Monday	**martes** *(martess)* Tuesday	**miércoles** *(meeyercolles)* Wednesday
	jueves *(hwebbess)* Thursday	**viernes** *(beeyernes)* Friday
	sábado *(sabbaddo)* Saturday	**domingo** *(domingo)* Sunday

The seasons

la primavera
(la preemaberra)
spring

el verano
(el beranno)
summer

el otoño
(el ottonyo)
autumn

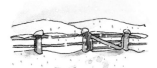

el invierno
(el inbeeyerno)
winter

julio
(hooleeyo)
July

agosto
(agosto)
August

septiembre
(septyembray)
September

octubre
(octoobray)
October

noviembre
(nobbyembray)
November

diciembre
(diceeyembray)
December

Clothes and parts of the body

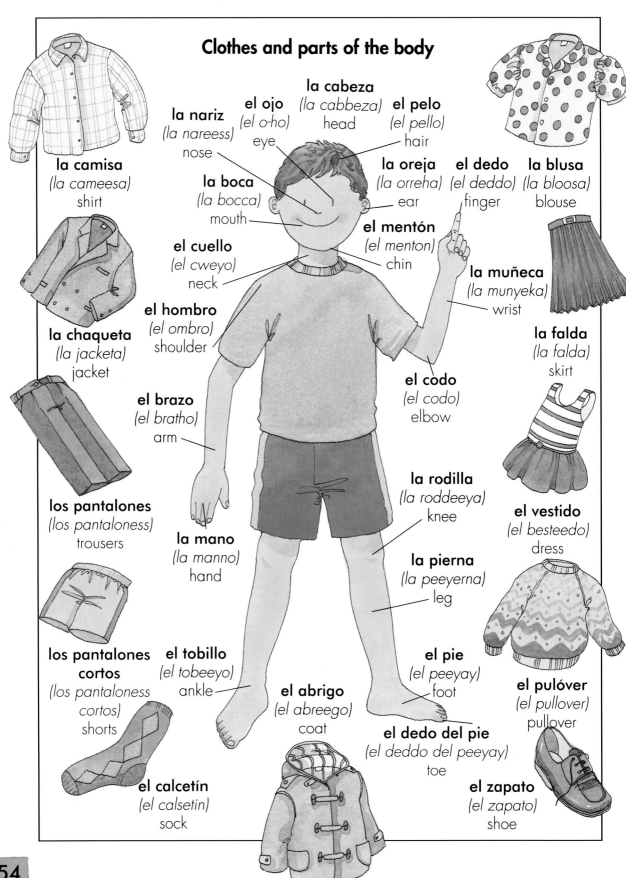

la camisa
(la cameesa)
shirt

la chaqueta
(la jacketa)
jacket

los pantalones
(los pantaloness)
trousers

los pantalones cortos
(los pantaloness cortos)
shorts

el calcetín
(el calsetin)
sock

la nariz
(la nareess)
nose

el ojo
(el o-ho)
eye

la cabeza
(la cabbeza)
head

el pelo
(el pello)
hair

la boca
(la bocca)
mouth

la oreja
(la orreha)
ear

el dedo
(el deddo)
finger

la blusa
(la bloosa)
blouse

el cuello
(el cweyo)
neck

el mentón
(el menton)
chin

la muñeca
(la munyeka)
wrist

el hombro
(el ombro)
shoulder

la falda
(la falda)
skirt

el brazo
(el bratho)
arm

el codo
(el codo)
elbow

la mano
(la manno)
hand

la rodilla
(la roddeeya)
knee

la pierna
(la peeyerna)
leg

el vestido
(el besteedo)
dress

el tobillo
(el tobeeyo)
ankle

el abrigo
(el abreego)
coat

el pie
(el peeyay)
foot

el pulóver
(el pullover)
pullover

el dedo del pie
(el deddo del peeyay)
toe

el zapato
(el zapato)
shoe

54

Colours and numbers

1 uno *(oono)*

2 dos *(doss)*

3 tres *(tres)*

4 cuatro *(cwattro)*

5 cinco *(seenko)*

6 seis *(seys)*

7 siete *(syettay)*

8 ocho *(ocho)*

9 nueve *(nwebbay)*

10 diez *(deeyes)*

11 once *(onsay)*

12 doce *(dosay)*

13 trece *(tresay)*

14 catorce *(catorsay)*

15 quince *(kinthay)*

16 dieciséis *(deeyeseeseys)*

17 diecisiete *(deeyeseesyettay)*

18 dieciocho *(deeyeseeocho)*

19 diecinueve *(deeyeseenwebbay)*

amarillo *(ammareeyo)* yellow

blanco *(blanco)* white

ocho — (see above)

naranja *(narranha)* orange

negro *(neggro)* black

rojo *(ro-ho)* red

Underneath is the Spanish verb tener, to have.

tengo *(tengo)* I have	**tenemos** *(tenemmos)* we have
tienes *(teeyennes)* you have (familiar singular)	**tenéis** *(tennayiss)* you have (familiar plural)
tiene *(teeyennay)* you have (polite singular) he/she/it has	**tienen** *(teeyennen)* you have (polite plural) they have

---

rosa *(rossa)* pink

gris *(greess)* gray

verde *(berday)* green

20 veinte *(beyntay)*

21 veintiuno *(beynteeoono)*

22 veintidós *(beynteedoss)*

30 treinta *(treynta)*

40 cuarenta *(cwarenta)*

50 cincuenta *(sinkwenta)*

60 sesenta *(sessenta)*

70 setenta *(setenta)*

80 ochenta *(ochenta)*

90 noventa *(nobbenta)*

azul *(azool)* blue

marrón *(marron)* brown

100 cien *(seeyen)*

1,000 mil *(meel)*

1,000,000 un millón *(oon meeyon)*

el cocodrilo
(el cocodreelo)
crocodile

Index

la ballena
(la bayena)
whale

el oso
(el osso)
bear

el lobo
(el lobo)
wolf

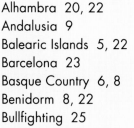

el delfín
(el delfeen)
dolphin

la panda
(la panda)
panda

la cebra
(sebra)
zebra

el tigre
(el tigray)
tiger

la gorila
(la goreela)
gorilla

el león
(el layon)
lion

el canguro
(el kangooroo)
kangaroo

el elefante
(el elefantay)
elephant

la jirafa
(la heeraffa)
giraffe